This Book Belongs To

Ella Bop
A Coloring Book For Married People

© 2013 Ella Bop
Outside The Lines Press

www.outsidethelinespress.com

ALL RIGHTS RESERVED

While there is no wrong way to propose to your girlfriend/boyfriend, there are less appropriate venues

Cheryl, will you marry me?

Yes!!!!

OMG! This is so cute! Congratulations you guys!

You two are the sweetest couple I know. Congrats!

Did you get down on one knee while typing this?

Match the unspoken assessment of your impending marriage with the corresponding friend or family member

Your judgemental aunt

"If he cheats, I will destroy him and everything he loves!"

"I guess she's off the market. For now."

Your unmarried older sister

"She must be pregnant. Why else is she marrying him?"

Your lecherous workmate

"I hate my life."

Your father

The lifelong probability of a marriage ending in divorce is approximately 50%

"Heads they make it, tails they don't. Don't blame me - the stats don't lie!"

"Do they stats also know that you're sleeping on the couch tonight?"

Help the married couple find their ideal honeymoon location

Hawaii

The groom's parents' sofabed

Jim's Trucker Motel, route 36 in Decatur, IL

These days, women are far less likely to take their husband's name

"So are you going to change your last name?"

"Well, my first name is Candy and his last name is Stohr. What do you think?"

A spouse's habitual use of smartphones or other handheld computing devices has been linked to marital tension

"There are three people in this marriage Peter. And one of them is at serious risk of getting chucked in the toilet."

The marriage bed is a private sanctuary for the married couple

Awkward conversations with your in-laws are an inevitable part of any marriage

"I have to admit, I was more than a little titillated when Ana first entered Christian's playroom and he showed her his toys."

"Oh my god, is your mother actually talking about 50 Shades of Grey right now? We have to go!"

Happily married people often do not realize that some folks are quite content being single

"So when are you going to find a man and settle down Julie? The clock is ticking!"

"If settling down means that my partner stops shaving or wearing deodorant, I think I'd rather stay single."

Frequency of lovemaking during a marriage progresses through four distinct stages

Daily

Weekly

Special occasions

"Let's wait until you get your new hip"

Having a hobby in common is an excellent way to stay connected with your spouse

"They come here every Sunday afternoon and spar for about an hour. And you know what? I've never seen a happier marriage."

One in ten women think men with moustaches are more attractive. Are you one of those women? To find out, cut out one of the below moustaches and tape it to your husband's upper lip while he's sleeping. Do you like what you see?

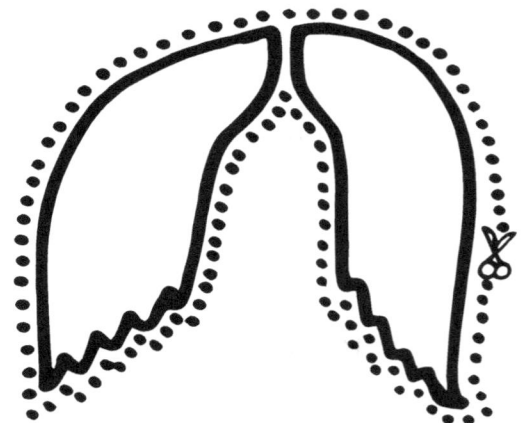

The male mid-life crisis can put a strain on even the best of marriages

"Hey Dawhin, did you know that Yong test drove a Miata this morning?"

"That's no big deal. Last week he got a nipple piercing, bought a paddle board, and sent in his application to NASA's astronaut training school."

A whirlwind romance in the couple's first few months to- gether often forms a rock-solid basis for a happy marriage

"Do you remem- ber our first kiss? We were dancing to this song in a romantic beach- side bar in Aruba when I took you in my arms and said..."

"I'm just gonna stop you right there. This is the story of when you first kissed Yvonne - your second wife. I'm Jennifer - remember? And the first time we kissed was after you said 'I bet your lips taste like that BBQ sauce you've been eating - mind if I check?'"

Sometimes you have to think outside of the box to solve marital problems

"This is Jim's solution to the problem of forgetting to put down the toilet seat. I'm fine with it."

Married People Word Find

```
W Q A P E F P B P P J J M M R Y I Z L J
A J K Z Z S L O V E F M P E K T B A T R
F Z G G P W Q Y I C Q L G K P R U Q B E
P B X I C R C M K D N E O U S D B Y S X
P R S N F S T H M D W E X W N F B C G Y
F Y G T B R C I S W A L N I E E F C M Z
X P N I A W E I X L Z D E H G R O P H D
T E I M Q Z P F T G E Y C E F M S Q M K
V Y P A J T S O J P W T H B P V K G C A
N F P C U R E V T X A O L R Z C N D H D
G Q I Y S Z R O B P S A O D L I Z S K V
N D L Q X E E C H Y U M V Y R T N R V A
I U C C E K V G D N I P Z W W D I F C B
R P L Y E G U V D S I K R Y H G W Y Z K
O P I U K O K R E X P V S E S V P P Y X
N U A B R Y Y K Z D R V M B S T T I Q S
S H N A I C L S Z A O S T K H E J J F D
K D E O K H F F T S H A R I N G N H Z N
P Q O F W Q N Y C G Y D V Q X F X T G O
C J T Z G Y J O D P H K O U Z E A W S V
```

compromise   intimacy

snoring   respect

love   laundry

flowers   presents

in-laws   sharing

rough patch   toenail clippings

At some point in the marriage, birthday presents stop being thoughtful gifts and start being subtle hints

"A nose hair trimmer?"

Eventually, you will have heard every amusing anecdote your partner has told at least once

"So then I say, Sheryl, I guess you **are** strong enough!!"

"What's wrong Josh?"

"Every time he tells that stupid story of how Sheryl Crow helped rescue him after he got stuck in a Porta Potty at Bonnaroo, I die a little inside."

Keeping the romance alive after decades of marriage requires a bit of effort

"I thought you said you got me flowers?"

"I did get you flour – I was hoping you'd bake me a Bundt cake this weekend."

The Married People Bedtime Cuddle Continuum

Year 1: fall asleep spooning each night

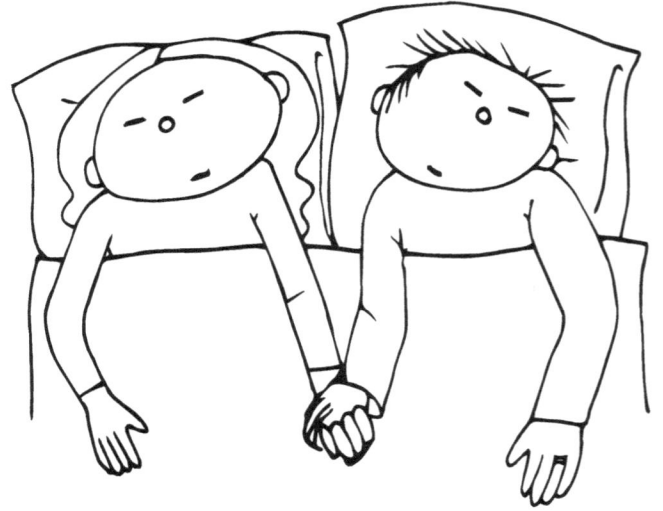

Year 5: fall asleep holding hands occasionally

Year 20: fall asleep facing opposite directions in a king sized bed

Year 40: fall asleep in separate bedrooms

Sticking by your spouse's side in good times or in bad is not always easy

"Hey honey, check out my new ink!"

"I know the pastor said 'for better or for worse,' but I think he'll make an exception for a face tattoo."

After years of marriage, spouses are so attuned to each other's needs that communication is seamless

"Frank! Did you hear a word I said? Just tell me where you left the vacuum cleaner!

"I think it was Bill Clinton."

Finding new ways to make your spouse feel loved and appreciated becomes increasingly challenging

Day 78 of the marriage

"I love the cute little way your nose crinkles when you laugh!"

Day 1278 of the marriage

"Thanks for clipping your toenails over the toilet for once!"

Modern appliances allow married couples to tackle household chores with minimal stress

"Just separate the silverware! It takes two seconds! Forks go with forks, spoons go with spoons… it's not rocket science!!!"

The underwear you put on in order to tempt your spouse into an evening of love-making passes through three stages over the course of the marriage

1st anniversary:
Sexy underwear

10th anniversary:
Slimming underwear

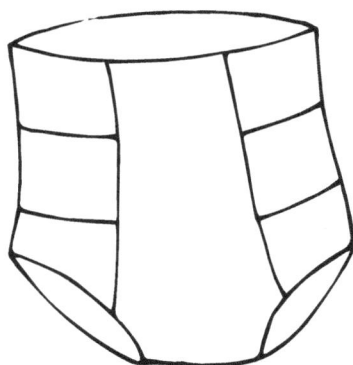

30th anniversary:
Clean underwear

Even after 30 years of marriage, you will still discover new things about your spouse that will surprise and delight you

"Will, is this your bow tie? I didn't know you had a bow tie."

"Was it in the box with my tear-away pants? That's from my old Chippendale outfit. Did I forget to mention that I was an erotic dancer before we met?"

Totally worth it

Special Thanks

This book was made possible thanks to the generous support of our Kickstarter campaign backers, including Will Cheung, Michael Teoh, and our dear friend Gen. Thanks to everyone who supported this project!

For more from the *Coloring Books for Adults series* from Outside The Lines Press, visit:

www.outsidethelinespress.com

Other titles in this series include:

A Coloring Book for Pregnant Ladies
A Coloring Book for New Parents

Coming soon:

A Coloring Book for Brides
A Coloring Book for Bridesmaids
A Coloring Book for Newlyweds
A Coloring Book for Dog Lovers
A Coloring Book for Cat Lovers
A Coloring Book for 30 Somethings

www.ingramcontent.com/pod-product-compliance
Lightning Source LLC
Chambersburg PA
CBHW081155040426
42445CB00015B/1892